Sasha Is a Good Citizen

Dominic Kawa

Infomax Readers

Rosen Classroom™

New York

Published in 2014 by The Rosen Publishing Group, Inc.
29 East 21st Street, New York, NY 10010

Book Design: Mickey Harmon

Photo Credits: Cover (flag) Kim Reinick/Shutterstock.com; cover (girl), p. 11 Studio Paggy/Getty Images; p. 5 Dennis Macdonald/Photolibrary/Getty Images; p. 7 Jon Feingersh/Blend Images/Getty Images; p. 9 larry1235/Shutterstock.com; p. 13 Binkski/Shutterstock.com; p. 15 Diego Cervo/Shutterstock.com; p. 17 Monkey Business Images/Shutterstock.com; p. 19 Stephen Finn/Shutterstock.com; p. 21 Kellie L. Folkerts/Shutterstock.com; p. 22 Oledjio/Shutterstock.com.

ISBN: 978-1-4777-2366-1
6-pack ISBN: 978-1-4777-2367-8

Manufactured in the United States of America

CPSIA Compliance Information: Batch #CS13RC: For further information contact Rosen Publishing, New York, New York at 1-800-237-9932.

Contents

What Is a Citizen?

Sasha lives in a busy town. That's where she goes to school and plays with her friends. Sasha's town is very nice, but there are rules she must follow almost everywhere she goes. In school, her class learned that following the rules is part of being a good citizen. Good citizens make our towns and cities better places to live.

What can you do to be a good citizen?
Read on to find out!

The LOON FEATHER
INDIAN CURIOSITIES GIFTS
PILOT HOUSE
RESTAURANT & PUB
Ryba's Fudge Sh
FERRY

Sasha's teacher told the class there are two kinds of American citizens. One is a person who was born in the United States. The other is a person from another country who becomes a citizen. Sasha was born in America. However, her grandma moved here from another country. Sasha's grandma became a citizen after she moved here.

People from other countries move to America so they can have a better life.

Rights and Duties

Sasha learned all American citizens have rights. That's one of the most important parts of living in our country. Citizens also have duties, and good citizens carry out their duties. Sasha's teacher said being a good citizen shows we're thankful to be in America. Sasha's homework was to find ways to be a good citizen in her town.

Our government made the laws that give American citizens our rights.

We the People
Article I.
JULY 4, 1776.
thirteen united States of

Helping at the Store

At the grocery store, Sasha saw an old woman with heavy bags of food. She could barely lift them! Sasha knew the woman needed help with her bags so she carried the bags for her. The woman was very happy that Sasha helped her. Helping an older adult is one way Sasha showed she's a good citizen.

Sasha helped the woman without being asked. It's a very nice thing to do.

Following the Rules

Then, Sasha went to the park. She had to cross the street to get there. There was a light that told her when it was safe to cross. Some people crossed the street without waiting for the light. Sasha knew that waiting for the light was the right thing to do. It shows that Sasha follows the rules. Good citizens always follow the rules.

Following the rules keeps everyone safe and happy!

DONT
WALK

Sharing

Sasha's friends were at the park when she got there. Sasha played with a ball. Her friend wanted to play with the ball, too. Sasha was happy to share it with her friend. This way, they both had fun! When Sasha shared with her friend, it showed she cared about him. Doing nice things for her friends is another way Sasha's a good citizen.

Sasha helped everyone have fun by sharing her ball.

When Sasha got home, her brother was teasing their sister. Sasha could tell it was hurting her sister's feelings. She told her brother to stop. This is called "standing up" for somebody. Sasha stood up for her sister because it's the right thing to do. Good citizens always try to help somebody when they're being picked on.

Standing up for others isn't always easy, but it's very important.

Sasha Volunteers

Good citizens show they **respect** Earth by **recycling**. On Sunday morning, Sasha **volunteered** at her town's recycling center. She sorted bottles, paper, glass, and cans into different bins. Recycling keeps Sasha's town clean. It keeps Earth healthy, too! Recycling makes Sasha's town a nice place to live.

Recycling is when we find different ways to use things we've used before.

RECYCLING POINT
PLASTIC BOTTLES ONLY
Food and drinks cans only
WASTE PAPER ONLY

Back in school, Sasha and her friends shared what they did to be good citizens. A lot of kids talked about helping the **elderly**, cleaning up their town, and being kind to one another. Being a good citizen made Sasha feel happy. She couldn't wait to do more things to help her community!

How have you been a good citizen where you live?

Are You a Good Citizen?

What do good citizens do?

- follow the rules
- keep their community clean
- pick up after themselves
- help neighbors and the elderly
- share with other people

Glossary

elderly (EHL-duhr-lee) Older adults.

recycle (rih-SY-kuhl) To use something again.

respect (rih-SPEHKT) To feel or show honor for.

volunteer (vah-luhn-TIHR) To do something to help because you want to do it.

Index